Con

C000039222

Walking times shown are approximate and depend on fitness, weight of rucksack, weather, conditions underfoot and height climbed.

Level of Difficulty **1** = Easy, **3** = Moderate, **5** = Hard
All walks are shown on O.S. Explorer map No.OL1 The Peak District – Dark Peak Area.
Every effort has been made to ascertain the accuracy of the walks described, the description of a route or track is not necessarily a right of way.

Some abbreviations have been used in the text to shorten it and make it more concise: -
PF = Public Footpath   RT = Right   LT = Left   FB = Footbridge
CP = Car Park   m = metres   km = kilometres   °M = magnetic
PB = Public Bridleway   RD = Road

Walkers are strongly advised to have the appropriate clothing and footwear for these walks.
- Boots/walking shoes.
- Waterproof Jacket.
- Over trousers.
- Small Rucksack for food, drinks and spare clothing.
- Hat & Gloves.
- Compass & map.

ISBN 978-1-903568-49-1

Walk 1 Castleton View Walk **Distance 3.5miles/5.6km**
Start GR. 149830 - Main CP in Castleton
Walk Time 2hrs

Terrain A good scenic walk with a short moderate ascent up Treak Cliff.

Leaving the main CP in Castleton, turn RT and walk to the CP for Peak Cavern, turning LT into it. At the far side cross a stone bridge over the stream. Turn RT and ascend the narrowing RD between the houses to where it ends (**1**). Continue on a stony track and go through a gate. Keep the stone wall on your RT as you follow a narrow path sweeping round to a gate leading onto the minor RD (**2**).

Cross the minor RD near Speedwell Cavern and go between two stone posts and continue on the obvious narrow path as you ascend towards Treak Cliff Cavern. Go up the steps to Treak Cliff Cavern then ascend another set of steps past it before turning immediately RT to walk behind the building on a narrow ascending path. Going through a gate, it takes you over the hillside and through another gate onto the topside of the hill.

On the top of the hill, walk across the open grass area to another gate by Blue John Cavern (**3**) then turn RT on the access RD. Walk round to the CP for the cavern on the minor RD. Turn RT and continue descending the RD past the parking places to a turning area.

Go through a small gate at the far side and follow the now disused RD, with care, down to another gate. Go through that gate and continue now straight ahead, going down a small stone track to Mam Farm (**4**). As you reach the farm courtyard, turn RT over a stile and follow the winding track round and over another stile as it gently descends.

You emerge in a small open area surrounded by trees where you bear LT across to another path in the direction of the cement works in the distance. As you descend cross a stile and go down a flight of steps then through a gate by the farm there. You emerge in front of Knowlegates Farm (**5**) and go through a small gate.

Cross a stone step stile then over another stile by a 5-bar gate, now heading into Castleton. At a cattle grid, do not cross, but walk to the far side of it and cross the stile. Keep the brook on your LT as you walk back into Castleton (**6**). At the RD, turn LT and walk along to the CP in Castleton.

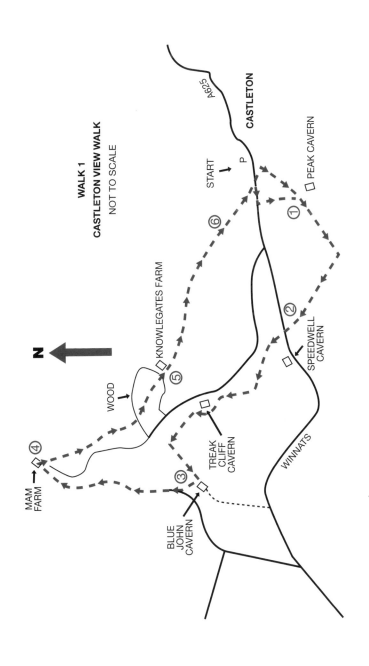

Walk 2 Castleton Hills Circular

Distance 3.9miles/6.3km

Walk Time 2hrs

Start GR. 149830 - Main CP in Castleton

Terrain A steep ascent followed by a steady walk over high ground then steep descent.

Leave the main CP in Castleton and cross to walk between the 3 Roofs Café and the Blue John Jewellers. Continue between the shops and houses then keep the stream on your RT as you walk to the small stone bridge a short distance further.

At the bridge continue walking along the RD, which narrows further up, then at the top, walk onto the stony track and continue past the trees, going through a gate onto a narrow path by a stone wall. Continue round the crescent shaped path then halfway round; look for a feint grass track branching steeply LT up the hillside (**1**).

Continue ascending to the top and turn RT near the wire fence and walk over the open grass to the RT of some crags with trees on them. Continue past the crags, now on flatter ground, to a farm gate at the far end of the large field. Cross a stone step stile at the side of the gate and walk up between the two broken stone walls. At the end of the broken walls, continue ahead ascending the field in the same direction.

You come to a wooden 5–bar gate (**2**) with an opening at the side. Go through then over a stone step stile soon after onto a track. Turn RT here on a stony track between two stone walls. When you come to a bend in the track, continue straight ahead following a PB sign through a metal farm gate. Go through another metal farm gate then when you come to a third, turn RT just before it, crossing a stile (**3**).

Walk diagonally across the field bearing 54°M over the undulating ground to steps over the wall, located about 60yds from the corner of the field. Walk in same direction through the next two fields until you emerge on an access track (**4**). Go through a metal farm gate on the track then over a ladder stile on your RT. A sign points to Castleton. Rowter Farm is just off to your LT now as you continue down the field.

Look ahead for a stile in the same direction and continue on the winding narrow grass path. Cross a step over a stone wall and continue on the grass path then over more stone steps. Keep a stone wall on your RT then cross a ladder stile. Walk directly to the tree at the far end of the field then to the steps over the wall by the nearby gate (**5**).

Continue over the next large field on your original track now going back to Castleton. Walk over the field in the direction of Castleton and the wood you may see ahead. You descend steeply now back on your original path down by the side of the wood then RT back along the stony path into Castleton.

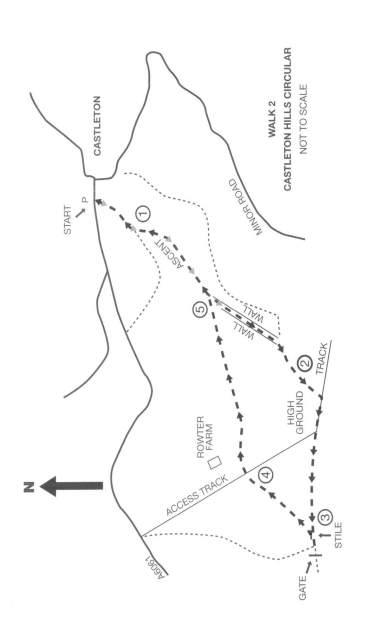

N

CASTLETON

START
P

①

② TRACK

③ STILE

④ ACCESS TRACK

⑤

WALL
WALL

ASCENT

MINOR ROAD

HIGH GROUND

ROWTER FARM

GATE

A6061

WALK 2
CASTLETON HILLS CIRCULAR
NOT TO SCALE

Walk 3 Castleton – Hope Riverside Walk   **Distance 4.1miles/6.6km**
Walk Time 1hr 45mins
Start GR. 149830 - Main CP in Castleton
**Terrain An easy flat circular walk over fields to Hope then by the river back
to Castleton.**

From the main CP in Castleton, turn LT and ascend by the row of shops to the sharp
bend by the Nags Head pub (**1**). Turn LT then at the next sharp bend continue ahead
along Back Street. Continue up the RD, passing houses on both sides. Where the RD
bears LT by an 'end of road' sign, you see Hollowford Centre (conference centre),
and just to the RT of that is a track with signs for Rotary and PF (**2**).

Walk along that track between the stone walls and at a cattle grid, cross and turn
immediately RT. Cross a field and some stepping stones over a brook then go through
a gate. Continue to a small gate just past a 5-bar gate. You come to the entrance to
Riding House Farm. Continue and go through a gate to emerge on a bend in the lane.
Turn LT at the bend then you come to a lane where there are five tracks all together
(**3**). Walk straight ahead then bear RT. Go through a 5-bar gate beside a house,
(which may be open), to emerge on a RD. A sign there states Lose Hill and Hope and
you turn LT on the one-track RD, going through a small gate at the side of a house.

Just through the gate, turn immediately RT, behind the stables and through two
small gates. Continue on the narrow path, which may be overgrown in parts. Go
through another small gate into a field and turn immediately LT and continue into
next field walking straight ahead to the far side. Go through a gate into next field
keeping the hedge line on your LT.

Go through another gate, over a small FB and ascend a short flight of steps to
another gate. Continue along the side of field with wire fence on RT side. Cross
another small FB and through another gate, keeping the fence on LT side. At a
wooden waymark post pointing to Hope, follow it across the field to a gate at the far
side. Go through a kissing gate and walk round the edge of the short field.

Walk through a gate onto a track, then through a metal gate following a PF sign.
Cross a stile then walk between the fence and hedge. At the end, go through a gate
and ahead in front of stone buildings onto a tarmac driveway. Pass a bungalow
walking ahead through a narrow opening and gate then over the railway bridge (**4**).
Emerging at the far side of a field, cross and go through a gate then through an
opening into next field. Keep in same direction over fields and through gates
following sign for Hope. Emerge on the RD with a school on your LT. Turn LT then
at the junction RT (**5**) to the main RD through Hope. Cross to walk down by the RT
side of the church for 300m. Continue down Tindale RD and ascend to a bench seat
on RT side. Cross the stile there to walk along by the river, crossing stiles and the
railway line (**6**) but stay in same direction.

Approaching Castleton, you see some houses as you follow the track to pass them
(**7**) and emerge on the RD in Castleton. Turn LT and walk back to the village centre
and CP.

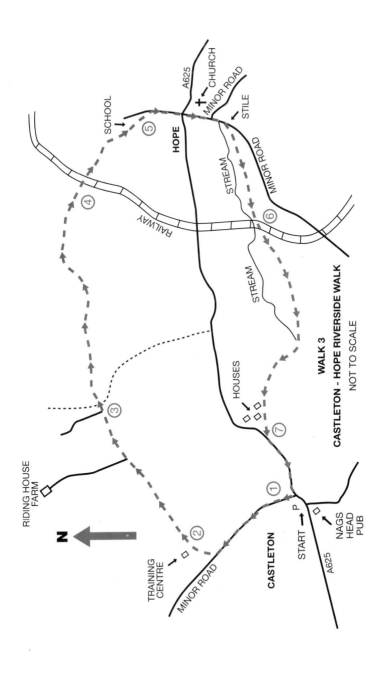

WALK 3
CASTLETON - HOPE RIVERSIDE WALK
NOT TO SCALE

Walk 4 Roman Road/Crookstone Hill   **Distance** 4.5miles/7.3km
Walk Time 1hr 50mins

Start GR. 168847 - Fullwood Stile Lane just off Townhead Bridge.

Terrain An excellent walk with a steep ascent followed by a walk on the old Roman road along the ridge. A gentle descent back to Townhead.

Park on Fullwood Stile Lane keeping well into the side to avoid blocking farm vehicles. Start from Townhead Bridge at the main RD and cross to the far side walking LT round the buildings to a sign to Lose Hill. Continue walking along the lane and take the RT fork (1) to pass a hotel. On reaching Oaker Farm cottages, take the PF to the LT of the cottages (2).

Cross two stiles there walking between the fences and over the fields. Continue in the same direction and cross the stile then bear RT down the track under the railway bridge to the RD. Cross the RD with care to cross a stile at the other side. Descend a path and follow it round and over Bagshaw Bridge (3).

Walk along the farm access RD and past Upper Fullwood Farm and the cottages there. Just past them, turn RT following the PF sign on a stony rutted track. Cross a stile then the track forks. Keep RT following the feint sign on a stone block there towards Crookstone Barn.

Ascend the grass and stony track then where the path forks again, take the LT fork ascending towards the clump of trees ahead and Crookstone Barn. The path narrows as you continue to ascend between the bracken and gorse. Cross a stile then at a broken stone wall ahead, turn RT (4) and ascend a stony track, going over a stile beside a metal gate and continue along the track, keeping the broken stone wall on your LT.

Approaching the trees of Woodlands Valley (5), turn RT over the stile following the sign to Win Hill and Hope then continue on a mostly gentle descent on the course of the old Roman road. You go through gates and ascend slightly before descending more steeply to Fullwood Stile Farm (6).

Approaching the farm, turn RT just before it, still staying on the access track, and continue descending, passing a white house on your LT then over the railway bridge. The track widens and becomes a metalled RD as you arrive at your original starting point.

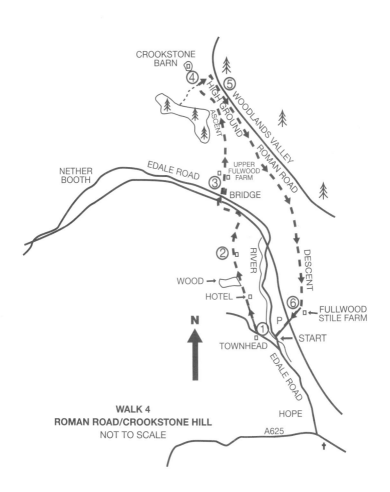

CROOKSTONE BARN

④

⑤

HIGH GROUND

ASCENT

WOODLANDS VALLEY

ROMAN ROAD

NETHER BOOTH

EDALE ROAD

UPPER FULWOOD FARM

③ BRIDGE

②

RIVER

WOOD →

HOTEL

DESCENT

⑥ FULLWOOD STILE FARM

P

① START

TOWNHEAD

EDALE ROAD

N

HOPE

WALK 4
ROMAN ROAD/CROOKSTONE HILL
NOT TO SCALE

A625

Walk 5 Lose Hill Viewpoint Walk   **Distance 4.9miles/7.9km**
Walk Time 2hrs 50mins
Start GR. 149830 - Main CP in Castleton
Terrain A steep ascent/descent of Lose Hill then generally a flat walk after, with good views.

From the main CP in Castleton, turn LT and ascend by the row of shops to the sharp bend by the Nags Head pub (**1**). Turn LT then at the next sharp bend continue ahead along Back Street. Continue up the RD, passing houses on both sides. Where the RD bears LT by an 'end of road' sign, continue up the lane. Where the lane bends round again, look for a wooden PF sign on your RT. Take this unmade track (**2**) towards Only Grange Farm. Turn up towards the farm through the double metal gates.

Further up follow the small yellow arrow beside two stone posts, crossing a stile there and keeping the hedge line just to your RT. Continue straight up to the farm, crossing the stiles, ahead. When you get to the farm, go over two stiles on the LT side of the farmhouse then ascend the steep hillside. Continue directly to the top of the hillside where there is a stile (**3**).

Turn immediately RT and walk on the stony path, which ascends, keeping the fence and wood to your RT. Continue to the compass point on the summit of Lose Hill then descend the slabbed path at the far side (**4**). On reaching a stile, cross then turn RT to another stile. Cross this and turn LT to descend a grass path towards some trees (**5**). You come to a sign pointing to Castleton. Turn RT here and follow it.

You go through a small gate and across the next field. At another signpost stating Castleton, turn RT here, crossing a double stile and keep in same direction to descend a faint grass path then join a track, which leads to Losehill Farm. You come to a metal gate with a stile by it and a yellow arrow on it. Cross the stile and continue ahead. Cross a step stile by a gate then turn LT to descend a stony track towards Riding House Farm.

Cross a stile and stay on the narrow path, descending a flight of steps then going through a gate. Turn LT on the path and cross a stile still on the path and near the brook and trees. Go through a kissing gate and turn RT along an access lane (**6**) and at the end of the lane is PF sign and an opening and a gate between two stones. Go through and continue along keeping the stone wall on your RT.

Go through a gate and cross stepping-stones over the brook then walk ahead over the field onto a farm access track. Stay in the same direction on the track to pass a training and conference centre. You emerge on the minor RD you originally started on. Turn LT and walk back into Castleton then RT at the main RD back to the CP.

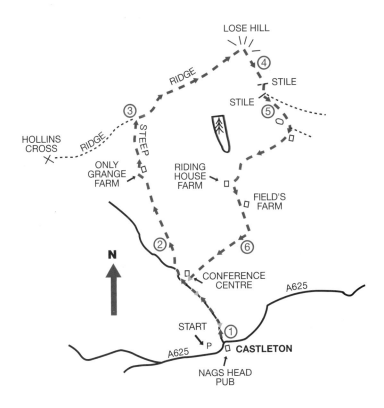

LOSE HILL

④

STILE

RIDGE

STILE

③

⑤

HOLLINS
CROSS

RIDGE

STEEP

ONLY
GRANGE
FARM

RIDING
HOUSE
FARM

FIELD'S
FARM

N

②

⑥

CONFERENCE
CENTRE

A625

START

①

P

A625   CASTLETON

NAGS HEAD
PUB

WALK 5
LOSE HILL VIEWPOINT WALK
NOT TO SCALE

Walk 6 Vale of Edale Walk   Distance 5.2miles/8.3km
Walk Time 2hrs 30mins

Start GR. 107847 - CP near railway bridge between Upper Booth and Barber Booth.

Terrain A pleasant walk with one main ascent/descent to Hollins Cross, good views along route.

From the CP near Barber Booth, walk back under the railway bridge and stay on the RD to the junction with a minor RD (**1**). Walk ahead onto a PF, crossing a stile at the RT of the stone bridge and continue in the same direction over fields and stiles. At a narrow strip of woodland, carry straight through in same direction and over more fields.

You emerge on an access lane at Harden Clough turn RT and walk up the lane to a sign on LT stating Hollins Cross (**2**). Go through the wooden gate and continue on a steady ascent through several gates to Hollins Cross. Your path merges with another just before the viewpoint (**3**).

At the viewpoint, bear LT on a stony path between a stone and wooden post in the direction of a row of houses and a mill, back into Edale Valley. Go through a gate, still descending, towards Backtor Farm then through another gate to pass the farm on the access RD (**4**). Follow the access RD as it winds round, crossing the bridge over the river to the main RD.

At the RD, turn RT walking, with care on the verge, for 150yds going under the railway bridge then turning LT (**5**) along a track, which leads to Woodhouse Farm. Go through the small gate at the entrance and continue on the track to the top where it bears LT. Follow it round then where the track goes over a cattle grid, go straight ahead through a small gate with a yellow arrow (**6**).

Cross a series of fields, then along an access track, still in the same direction, passing houses at Nether Ollerbrook then Middle Ollerbrook. When you reach the last farm building the path forks, take the LT path along a track to descend into Edale. You should see the tower of Edale church ahead (**7**).

On reaching the RD through Edale, turn LT, walking past the campsite. Look for a PF sign on your RT that leads along the front of a row of cottages (**8**). Walk in front of the cottages then over a stile on your LT, taking you over the fields through openings and gates. As you approach the railway bridge (**9**), turn LT down the track taking you over the bridge and descend to the houses at Barber Booth.

Turn RT to the stone bridge over the river at the far side of the houses, then RT at the other side walking back along the lane where you started from, back to the CP.

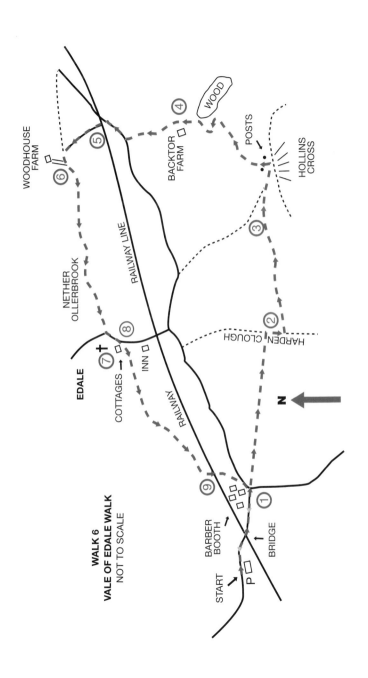

WALK 6
VALE OF EDALE WALK
NOT TO SCALE

WOODHOUSE FARM

EDALE

NETHER OLLERBROOK

COTTAGES

INN

RAILWAY LINE

RAILWAY

BACKTOR FARM

WOOD

POSTS

HOLLINS CROSS

HARDEN CLOUGH

N

BARBER BOOTH

BRIDGE

START

P

① ② ③ ④ ⑤ ⑥ ⑦ ⑧ ⑨

Walk 7 Caverns View Circular Walk   **Distance** 6.2miles/10km
Walk Time 3hrs 45mins
Start GR. 149830 - Main CP in Castleton.

Terrain A good walk with fascinating scenery and excellent views. One steep ascent/descent and one steady ascent.

From the main CP in Castleton, turn LT and ascend by the row of shops. Turn RT just past the Nags Head pub on your RT, and walk past the village green keeping LT by The Cosy Cottage tearoom then RT following the sign to Cave Dale. Walk between the narrow rock faces (1) and through a gate before ascending the hillside on a narrow stony path.

Continue ascending to the top where you see a stone wall on your RT side. Approaching the top, you see a gate (2) on your RT which you go through, walk on the path to go through another gate. You come to a broken stone wall on your RT, which you walk alongside. When the wall stops, bear to your RT to walk alongside another stone wall (3) in same direction.

After 100yds you come to a wooden 5–bar gate with an opening at the side. Go through then over a stone step stile soon after onto a track. Turn RT here on a stony track between two stone walls. When the track bends RT (4) continue straight ahead following a PB sign through a metal farm gate.

Go through this gate then when you come to another, turn RT just before it, crossing a stile to ascend the field keeping a stone wall on your LT side (5). At the far LT corner of the field, cross a stone step stile into next field and descend this field still keeping the stone wall on your LT. Follow the cut grass path and as you reach lower ground, you see a RD ahead.

You come to a white gate (6) leading onto the RD. Turn RT then LT going through a small gate by the 5-bar gate. Keep the stone wall on your LT as you ascend towards Mam Tor and the 'V' shape in the hillside. Stay on the main track then go through another small gate onto the main A625 RD (7). Cross diagonally LT to go through another wooden gate to ascend the grass path to the summit, going up a flight of steps.

On reaching the RD at the top, bear RT through a small gate, ascending steps to the summit of Mam Tor. Passing the 'trig' point, stay on the ridge (8) to Hollins Cross (round stone monument) then bear RT down the hill on a narrow stone slabbed path (9) which bends round. Look for the farm lower down on the RT as you descend and go through a gate. Take the short path bearing off RT taking you near the farm (10).

On the farm access track, go straight across through two small wooden gates and along the side of fields keeping the hedge line on your RT. Go through another gate then across a small FB. Cross two stiles together, bearing LT keeping a small wood on your LT side (11). Cross a stile by a farm gate onto an access RD. Turn RT over the stream then LT following a PF to Castleton via 'The Flatts'. Continue towards Castleton keeping the stream on your LT. Go through an opening and over several fields towards the houses ahead.

Walk through the opening between the houses onto the RD. Turn LT on the RD taking you back to the CP.

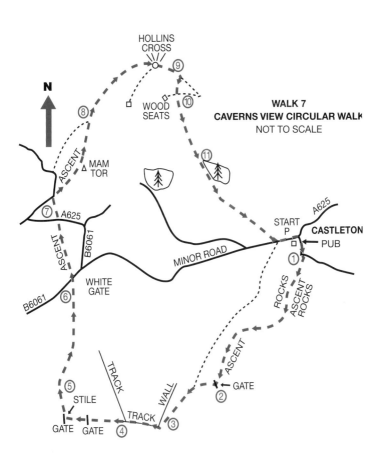

N

HOLLINS CROSS

⑨

⑧

WOOD SEATS

⑩

WALK 7
CAVERNS VIEW CIRCULAR WALK
NOT TO SCALE

ASCENT

MAM TOR

⑪

⑦

A625

START P

A625

CASTLETON

ASCENT

B6061

MINOR ROAD

PUB

①

ROCKS

ASCENT

ROCKS

WHITE GATE

⑥

B6061

TRACK

WALL

ASCENT

GATE

②

⑤

STILE

TRACK

GATE   GATE   ④   ③

Walk 8 Jacobs Ladder

Distance 6.3miles/10.1km

Walk Time 3hrs 15mins

Start GR. 107847 - CP between Upper Booth and Barber Booth

Terrain A good walk with a short but steep ascent then a long gentle descent back.

Turn LT from the CP walking to Upper Booth (**1**). As you near the farm buildings there, continue on the narrow RD following sign for Jacobs Ladder. Cross the small bridge there and ascend the narrow RD. Go through a small gate next to a 5-bar gate following sign for Lee Farm. Stay on the access RD to the farm. On reaching the farm buildings, continue between them onto the rough stony track (**2**).

Cross two stiles next to 5-bar gates as you ascend the valley before coming to a gate beside a stone FB over the stream. Cross then ascend the stone stepped path known as Jacobs Ladder (3). At the top of the hill you come to a 5-bar gate with the Pennine Way on your RT and a step stile by the gate. Cross then turn immediately LT (**4**) onto a slabbed path continuing over the top of the hillside by a broken stone wall.

Just over the brow of the hill is another path turning off LT (**5**). Turn LT and walk to the 'trig' point on the highest ground at Brown Knoll then on a gradual descent over a wide expanse of open hillside. Follow the worn peat path now over level ground, which can be wet and boggy in places. You see a tower ahead, which is a ventilation shaft. Keep it well off to your RT as you pass, still on the path (**6**).

You join a track near a wooden post. Bear LT on this track (**7**), which soon bends round to the RT on a rutted track and descends the hillside going through a small gate by a 5-bar gate. Cross a step stile by another 5-bar gate then immediately LT through a small opening by a gate following a yellow arrow. Cross a small field diagonally, go over a stile and through a gate as you descend towards the derelict building in the valley. Behind it is Manor House Farm (**8**).

After crossing two stiles you come to an access track leading to the farm. Turn LT and walk to the railway bridge over the minor RD. At the RD, turn LT and walk back to the CP.

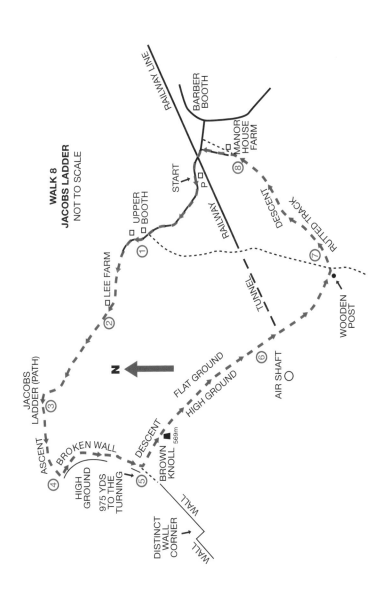

WALK 8
JACOBS LADDER
NOT TO SCALE

Walk 9 Rushup Ridge/Hollins Cross Circular Walk   Distance 8.1miles/13.1km
Walk Time 3hrs 30mins
Start GR. 124853 - Main CP in Edale
Terrain A good undulating walk with excellent views and one steep ascent/descent.

Turn RT from the main CP in Edale and walk under the railway bridge into the village. On reaching the Old Nags Head pub, turn LT, following a sign for Upper Booth (1).

Go through a kissing gate then another gate further up as you ascend the path. You come to a stile on LT, signposted for Upper Booth. Cross and walk on a slabbed path, going through two openings into fields (2). Cross stone steps over the wall into a further field.

Continue around the hillside through a small wooden gate on the obvious path then over stone steps again. At a sign for Crowden Clough/Jacobs Ladder, follow Jacobs Ladder LT. Descend the hillside, cross a stile then through a small gate, still descending gently into the valley.

Cross a stile, continue on the rutted track crossing another stile by a 5-bar gate. You are now at Upper Booth (3) as you walk between the farm buildings and descend the winding path between them and past a post box. At the lower end of the farm go straight across on a narrow path just to the RT of the telephone box.

Cross a small FB into a copse and ascend the far side to cross a stile out of it. You emerge in a grass field with a farm ahead. A stone step stile is just to the RT of it. Cross then bear RT up the embankment to a gate. Continue across the next field to a metal farm gate by a barn. Keep the stone wall on your LT as you cross the undulating hillside and drop down to a ladder stile.

Cross and descend by a wood, keeping the stone wall just to your LT. Cross fields and two further stiles approaching the railway line/tunnel. At a house called 'The Orchard' (4) you drop down to cross the FB and over a stile onto an unmade track.

Cross the track following a sign for Whitemoor Clough, through a small gate keeping the stone wall just to your LT. Cross a stile where your path bends RT then LT, to cross a brook. Stay on path to a stile leading into a field with a barn. Walk to far side of the barn and cross a stile. You are now at the base of a hill. Ascend the hill; you come to a rutted track after a short distance.

Turn RT on this track and follow it to the ridge along the top of the hill. Another track joins from the RT but continue ahead. On meeting a definite path (5), running RT to LT, turn LT and follow this path for 1.7miles and cross a stile to emerge on a RD between the hillsides (6). Turn LT then RT at a bus stop and go through a gate following a rutted track up the hillside. Your path merges with the path descending from the summit.

Go through a gate onto a stone slabbed path and continue to a round stone structure at Hollins Cross. Turn sharp LT onto a path towards Edale, 100m further is another path (7), but stay on the RT hand one descending to Edale, in the valley ahead.

Pass to the LT of a house and through a gate onto a farm access track. Follow this track descending to a stile and crossing the stream. Ascend to the minor RD (8) and then turn LT on the RD, walking back 450m to the CP.

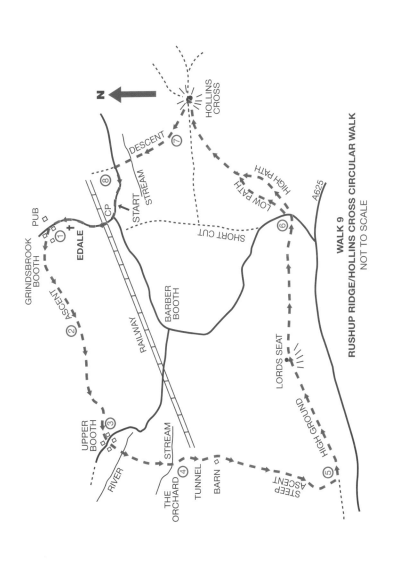

N

WALK 9
RUSHUP RIDGE/HOLLINS CROSS CIRCULAR WALK
NOT TO SCALE

GRINDSBROOK
BOOTH

PUB

EDALE

① ASCENT ②

RAILWAY

BARBER
BOOTH

UPPER
BOOTH

③

RIVER

STREAM

THE
ORCHARD

TUNNEL

④

BARN

STEEP
ASCENT

⑤

HIGH GROUND

LORDS SEAT

⑥

A625

LOW PATH

HIGH PATH

HOLLINS
CROSS

⑦

DESCENT

STREAM

START

CP

⑧

SHORT CUT

Notes